Life and Survival

THE LADYBIRD

Cécile Duval

FRANKLIN WATTS
in association with
TWO-CAN

They look very large here . . .

Spring at last

Under the gentle warmth of the sun, the meadow is covered in flowers. The buzzing of the bees mingles with the first birdsong of the year.

A cautious butterfly leaves the head of a daisy to settle down a little further off. In the heart of another large yellow flower, two ladybirds are peacefully sunbathing. Nothing scares them. When ladybirds are in danger they squirt out a bitter fluid, so foul-smelling and evil-tasting that their enemies soon learn to avoid them. Those birds, rodents and spiders that have already met this nasty liquid will never forget the experience and find it's best to leave the ladybirds alone.

. . . but a ladybird is really about the same size as a coffee bean.

Seven dots doesn't mean seven years old

Even if a ladybird has seven spots on its back, that does not mean that it is seven years old. The fact is that such a ladybird is no older than its cousin with two spots. The number of spots on a ladybird's back have nothing to do with its age: it is actually a distinguishing feature between the different types of ladybird. There are over 3,000 species in the world.

If we look a little closer, we can see that the back is not a single carapace, or hard shell; it separates in the middle. In fact, these are two hard wings, known as elytrons, which protect the ladybird from parasites and from drying out.

The seven-spotted ladybird cannot mate with its two-spotted neighbour because they are completely different species.

The ladybird does not show its flat stomach often. Like all other insects, it has six legs and a segmented body. When it senses danger it pretends to be dead and stops moving.

It's difficult to find the little black eyes of a ladybird: they are next to the white patches.

Ladybird, ladybird, fly away home

The ladybird beats its wings many times every second to move about in the air: it is very difficult to see it flying. It often flies long distances, especially in good weather. Its favourite temperature is between 15°C and 25°C (60°F–75°F).

The ladybird reaches the top of the flower and lifts its red and black wingcases.

It unfolds its transparent wings and flies away at a terrific speed.

Soon the male leaves in search of a female. He circles around her, then comes close and climbs on her back to mate: not an easy feat on a slippery, round back.

After they have mated, the seven-spotted ladybirds wander into the low grasses, cereal crops, beetroot or rape. What can they be looking for?

It's difficult to tell male and female ladybirds apart, except when they are mating, when the male mounts the female.

Scourge of the aphids

The female ladybird examines the stalks of plants for any sign of her favourite food: aphids. She must build herself up before laying her eggs. She is a true predator, and will eat over 15 species of aphid.

A ladybird can eat up to 100 aphids a day: it will eat even more than that if it chooses only the juiciest parts.

Aphids cause terrible damage to plants by clustering around the stems. They weaken the plant by sucking out the sap, and sometimes spread disease to it.

Ladybirds bite aphids on the thigh, then make the flesh tender by injecting it with saliva before chewing them with their powerful jaws.

Sometimes the ladybird will suck out the insides of an aphid, which then deflates like a balloon.

Out of the 90 species of ladybirds that live in Britain, only four species are phytophagous, which means that they eat plant matter, like the one shown above.

Not all ladybirds share this diet. Some prefer to eat caterpillars, others like mushrooms and some feed on plants. Even those which eat aphids in the spring will feed on other insects, nectar or pollen during the summer.

The female searches carefully for the aphid colonies where she will lay her eggs.

The eggs are the size of a pinhead, and are easy prey for many other insects.

A ladybird can lay between 50 and 1,000 eggs during her lifespan. This depends on the type of ladybird, on the food available to the adult, and on the climate. The black aphids, next to the eggs, have no idea what is in store for them.

Golden eggs

One to two weeks after mating when the female ladybird has eaten a huge number of aphids, she will lay her eggs. She does this either within an aphid colony or close to one, because she knows that the small larvae will also welcome the feast. One by one, she glues her eggs vertically in groups below the leaves. On average, she lays 50 eggs a day, but the number depends on how many aphids are available for food.

Four days later when the larvae are ready to hatch, the eggs crack at the tip and small legs appear. The larva dries out before it goes hunting.

The eggs are a golden yellow when first laid, and later become greenish in colour. Then the larvae emerge head first: they are small and transparent and are still very delicate.

Huge appetites

The larvae hungrily devour the sugary aphids. They are at first smaller than their prey, but then grow very quickly. As it grows, the larva wriggles and crawls out of its skin, which has become too tight. It emerges in a larger skin, which will give it more room to grow.

The larva is now over one centimetre (one-third inch) long, and has shed its skin four times in 18 days. It eats even more than an adult ladybird, devouring about 100 aphids a day.

Ants also take an interest in aphids, because they love the aphids' sugary nectar. In exchange for this tasty food, they tend the aphids like farmers and protect them against the ladybirds and their larvae.

This winged aphid is a real find: the blind larva manages to locate its prey by moving about on the plant's stem, or along the veins and edges of the leaves.

An ant milks an aphid for nectar at the end of its abdomen by tapping it on the stomach with its antennae; a drop is released, and the ant sucks it up immediately.

The ant, angry at being disturbed, bites the ladybird larva with its sharp jaws, and injects it with poison. The wounded larva drops onto the ground: a lucky escape.

An extraordinary change

Three weeks later, the larva stops eating. It is now large enough to become an adult, but it must undergo one last change before it turns into a ladybird.

The larva attaches itself to a plant with a sort of foot at the end of its abdomen.

It changes into a chrysalis without moving at all. Inside this stiff dry nymph, the future ladybird is developing.

At the end of eight days, the ladybird begins to move. Suddenly it gives a shake, tears the nymph case, and comes out head first.

The new ladybird is yellow all over and has no spots. It turns around and chooses an open space on the stem to rest, and to allow its body to harden.

The ladybird's wingcases, at first dull and supple, soon become shiny. Without lifting its transparent wings, it unfolds them to dry . . .

. . . and small black spots gradually appear on its back.

The ladybird's last cast-off skin is now no more than a small empty sac next to its new body.

The young ladybird sets off to hunt aphids as soon as it can move about: it must build up its reserves of fat and sugar.

These two ladybirds are different colours because they are different ages. The redder they are, the older they are.

Beautiful and new

As if by magic the ladybird slowly takes on an orange colour, and the black spots on its back are now well defined. It eats constantly until the start of the summer when all the aphids are gone, then it eats other insects.

Only 20 per cent of all the young ladybirds that emerge in the spring survive the attacks of their many enemies: predators, parasites and disease.

Time to go

When the hot weather comes, the seven-spotted ladybird loses its appetite, and sets off on its migration with its companions. It leaves the meadows and heads for higher lands, helped on its journey by the summer winds.

The ladybird may stop at the seaside or on the edge of a hill; it may also land on a tower, a house or a tree, as long as it can find a raised and open position. Here it will group together with hundreds of other ladybirds of the same species to rest during the autumn and winter.

During their migration ladybirds can fly for 50 km (30 miles) without stopping, and will sometimes fly as high as 2,000 m (6,500 feet).

In winter ladybirds shelter grouped together under stones, in the cracks of rocks, or in the bark of trees. When they wake again, they have used up all their stores of energy and are much lighter.

Above all, ladybirds need a warm and dry climate. Certain plants, such as pine, juniper, box and broom, are good resting places if the winter is not too harsh.

Many ladybirds die in epidemics spread by a few diseased individuals. Those that survive will wake in January, but they will wait for warm weather before breeding once more, and again eating the aphids.

Depending on how much space is available, ladybirds gather to spend the winter in groups of between ten and several thousand.

Protect ladybirds and protect our plants

The ladybird is the scourge of aphids and the friend of the forester and the farmer, but it is very vulnerable. How can we help it to survive and multiply for the sake of our environment?

The ladybirds bred on marrows and watermelons at Antibes were released in Mauritania and Morocco in the fight against the caterpillars that feed on the date palm.

Avoid using insecticides

Ladybirds die when they come into contact with vegetation treated with insecticides and when they eat poisoned insects. Their eggs and larvae are directly destroyed by these chemical products.

Building artificial shelters

When placed at the foot of plants where ladybirds come to gather for the winter, artificial shelters of fibro-cement resembling the cracks in rocks help ladybirds to stay alive during the cold months. This helps build up the number of these useful insects.

An artificial shelter placed in the hills of upper Provence in France, by the scientists of the National Institute of Agricultural Research in Antibes.

The breeding station at Antibes

Scientists at the biological research station at Antibes in France have created a mass breeding programme of the different species of ladybird that are useful to the forester and farmer. Some species are native to America, Australia or Africa: these are released at the right moment in the South of France and in Africa to combat the ravages of caterpillars. Scientists are actively searching for ways to improve this struggle between insects.

The breeding apparatus at Caen. On the lower shelf, the black aphids multiply while eating the stalks of broad beans growing on damp wood shavings. The ladybird eggs are placed in nylon cages on the shelf above; the cages are closed off but aerated, and contain broad beans covered with aphids. The larvae then turn into adult ladybirds.

Insect against insect

Every spring, farms are invaded by aphids which destroy the crops. Using chemical controls creates serious problems, because many other animals die.

To protect the farms by limiting the numbers of aphids, scientists decided to use ladybirds which eat huge amounts of the pests. First of all it is necessary to breed the ladybirds in large quantities before releasing them into the wild, so that there are enough to perform this vital task. This is called biological warfare.

An experiment at Caen

Since 1981, the French town of Caen has established a breeding programme for seven- and two-spotted ladybirds to fight the infestations of aphids. Scientists begin by raising aphids to feed to the ladybirds, which multiply in large numbers at the laboratory. The scientists then release the ladybirds into the town. Caen no longer uses insecticides against aphids because of this method.

The ladybird family

There are more than 3,000 species of ladybird in the world, of which there are 90 species in Britain and Europe. They make a very colourful show: red ones, black ones, and yellow ones, with two, seven, fourteen or twenty-two spots on their backs.

The *sixteen-spotted ladybird* looks very elegant in its pink and black shell.

The *two-spotted ladybird* is very common. It is red with black spots . . .

. . . or black with red spots. The two individuals can reproduce together because they belong to the same species, just like people with different coloured hair.

These mating ladybirds are vegetarian: they love to eat melon leaves.

This *variable-spotted ladybird* eats aphids as eagerly as its seven-spotted cousin.

These are *fourteen-spotted ladybirds.* The male, black with yellow spots, mounts the female who is yellow with black spots.

Just to be different, some ladybirds have no spots at all . . .

. . . while others have many. This ladybird is African and comes from Uganda. There's so much variation in one family!

INDEX

First published in this edition in 1990 by
Franklin Watts
96 Leonard Street
London EC2A 4RH

English translation by Monica Byles

A CIP Cataloguing record for this book is available from the British Library ISBN 0-7496-0375-5

Printed in Belgium by Casterman, SA

Photographs © Anne and Jacques Six except:
JACANA: Collobert p 4, Pilloud p 6 (bottom), p 9, Veiller p 11, Tercafs p 14 (top), Dulhoste p 15 (top), Winner p 15 (bottom), Roux p 22 (top), Nardin p 7 (bottom right), p 22 (bottom), Rebouleau p 23 (top); FOTOGRAM STONE: p 6-7 (background), Berne p 16-17 (background); DOUGIN: p 25 (bottom); STAROSTA: p 14 (bottom); BOULOUX: p 23 (bottom); INRA: Iperti p 24-25, p 24 (bottom); CHAUBET: p 19 (bottom right)